# WALK
## ON THE
# MOON

## by Stephanie Moy

Orlando   Boston   Dallas   Chicago   San Diego

Visit *The Learning Site!*

www.harcourtschool.com

Look up at the moon at night. It is a big, beautiful, glowing ball. What is it like on the moon? What would it be like to visit? Many people have asked these questions, but only a small number of people have ever walked on the moon. They were all astronauts, people who travel in space.

On July 20, 1969, Neil Armstrong stepped on the moon. He was the first person to do it. There are many famous pictures of astronauts on the moon. They pose for the pictures and hold a United States flag.

The moon looks as if it is close to us. Some nights it looks so close that you could reach up and touch it. The moon is our closest neighbor, but it's still very far away. It's about 240,000 miles from Earth. It would take three days to travel to the moon in a rocket. The moon is also much smaller than Earth. About 49 moons could fit inside Earth!

The moon orbits, or travels around, Earth. It takes about one month for the moon to go around Earth.

    The moon is not like Earth. There is no water
on the moon, and there are no plants or living
things. The rocky ground is covered with gray
dust. It is very dusty. If you walked on the moon,
you would have to brush dust from your hair
and your clothes. You would have dust caked in
your mouth, and dust in your nose. You would
also shiver in the cold and bake in the heat. The
temperature on the moon can be 260°F. during
the day and -280°F. during the night.

There is also no atmosphere on the moon. The atmosphere is a group of gases around a planet. This means there is no wind, weather or air to breathe. Without air, sound cannot travel. That means you can't hear anything on the moon. The sky is always black, too. Even during the day, you could see stars shining in the sky.

The moon has less gravity than Earth does. Gravity is what makes things fall to the ground. With less gravity, people and things are lighter. They weigh less. You probably couldn't walk on the moon. You would have to float.

Scientists had to think about all these things when they made plans for people to visit the moon. How could people breathe? What would they eat? How could they walk around?

Animals went into space before humans did. Scientists wanted to see if living things could go to the moon and come back alive. The country known as the Soviet Union sent a dog named Laika into space. The United States sent a chimpanzee named Ham into space. Scientists learned from those missions. They decided that people could go into space, too.

Scientists made special clothing called spacesuits for astronauts. First came a soft shirt and pants. There was water inside them to cool the astronaut's body. Next came more clothing to keep out the heat and cold. Astronauts also wore helmets and gloves to protect their faces and hands. The spacesuits were huge and very heavy: They weighed about 180 pounds on Earth. On the moon, they weighed only about 30 pounds. That is because there is less gravity on the moon.

On July 16, 1969, a rocket ship, or space-craft, named *Apollo 11* took off to visit the moon. On board were three astronauts. Their names were Michael Collins, Neil Armstrong, and "Buzz" Aldrin. They were the first men to walk on the moon. Their trip was to gather information about the moon. They took photographs and gathered rocks. The astronauts also set up experiments. They wanted to know more about the moon.

Their spacecraft had two parts. Armstrong and Aldrin were in the tiny part called the *Eagle*. This was the part that landed on the moon. Collins was in the larger part, called the *Columbia*. This part of the spacecraft orbited the moon while the other two astronauts walked on the moon.

The astronauts would spend many days in the dark of space. The only lights were the ones inside the two spacecrafts. They would talk through a radio to people on Earth and with each other.

Neil Armstrong was the first man to walk on the moon. As he stepped onto the moon, he said, "That's one small step for a man... one giant leap for mankind." It's a good thing he had a spacesuit. Without it, no one would have heard him. There's no sound on the moon.

Armstrong and Aldrin were on the moon for about three hours. They picked up moon rocks, found out what the temperature was, and took pictures to show to people back on Earth. Their trip was very important. There were stories in newspapers all over the world. Some of their photos are in museums.

After *Apollo 11*, six other spacecraft went to the moon. More people walked on the moon. Astronauts picked up more moon rocks. They explored more of the landscape, and set up more experiments. They did this so that scientists on Earth could learn more about how the moon was formed. They wanted to learn what the moon was made of and how old it was. There are plans to visit the moon in the future. Someday astronauts may build a base there. This would allow more people to come to the moon.

Astronauts learned a lot about walking on the moon. At first they were afraid to walk very fast or very far. They were scared that their spacesuits might not work. But soon they learned to walk quickly. Because there is less gravity on the moon, they could jump high and take long steps.

It was also very easy to throw and carry things on the moon. Astronaut Alan Shepard hit a golf ball almost 200 yards on the moon!

Some things were harder to do in space. It was hard for the astronauts to bend over in their spacesuits. To pick up rocks, they had to use a special stick with a hook on the end.

It was also hard to sleep at night. Some astronauts slept in their spacesuits because it was hard to put them on and take them off. The astronauts were uncomfortable. It was hard to sleep.

Many things were hard to do. Simple activities that you could do on Earth could not be done on the moon.

There also was no gravity in the spaceship either. The astronauts had to learn new ways to do things. The astronauts could not brush their teeth like they did on Earth. With no gravity, the water floated away. When the astronauts ate, their food flew around the spacecraft. Astronauts had to strap themselves into bed at night so they wouldn't float around while they were sleeping. Their clothes, their shoes, and eyeglasses would slip from their hands. These things would float around the ship.

New information was found on each trip to the moon. Scientists studied some of the problems the astronauts had. Scientists then made new things for later trips. Scientists found new ways to help the astronauts. One of those things was a small car that could ride over the rocky, dusty ground on the moon. It went much more slowly than a real car. The ride was very bumpy, but there were no other cars. The astronauts had to wear seat belts anyway.

No one has walked on the moon since 1972. Twelve astronauts touched the dusty, rocky moon surface in that mission. They drove the moon car one last time, and looked at stars in the daytime.

Because there is no wind or water on the moon, their footprints are still there. They will stay there until some new astronauts make new footprints.

There are more plans for moon exploration. Someday there will be more footprints. Who will be the next person to walk on the moon? Maybe it will be you.